The Advent of Romance

Makeem White

Can you "fertilize the garden?"

Table of Contents

CHAPTER ONE

"Hi," a young man says to a girl. "You wanna go catch a movie with me?"

"I'm sorry, Toni," the girl replies, "I can't go with you. I already have a boyfriend."

"Oh," Toni sighs. "Okay then... I'll see ya later."

"Bye, Toni."

Toni sees the girl walk away, going back to her friend's table.

"First the B-Walk, now the Outcline?" Antonio thinks to himself. He proceeds to walk to a table, with a blond male already sitting there, waiting for him.

"Yo, Toni!" the blond shouts. "How'd it go?"

"Not good, Joey," Toni shouts back. He sits at the table Joey's at, with a DC Cola in his hand.

"I'm sorry to hear that, man."

"It's no big deal... So, how's your day going?"

"Pretty good, Toni," Joey says as he eats a French fry. "No complaints as usual. How about yours?"

"Well, besides the fact that I can't get a date," Toni starts, "I'm just out here, living the dream." He takes a sip of his DC Cola. "Hey, remember Czar Wars?"

"Yeah, those movies were awesome!"

"Remember that girl 'Zyubaqua?'" Toni asks. "You dated her, like, eons ago."

"Yeah," Joey replies, "She had those big, bushy eyebrows that I loved so much."

"I forgot about that part…"

"You remember who I dated after that?"

"Which one?" Toni asks. "There were so many..."

"Good question… there's been quite a few over the years. Guess they weren't meant to be…" Joey eats another French fry.

"It never seems to be a problem for you..." Toni says.

"True, but it's starting to get old, if you know what I mean." Joey replies.

"I don't. Remember, I never had a girlfriend."

"I keep forgetting about that…"

"It's all good because I will find *the* one someday!" Toni boldly states.

"Speaking of someday," Joey transitions, "remember when we wanted to go to Purrassic Park?"

"Purrassic Park, how could I forget about that?! It was the childhood dream!"

"Your mom got you one of those toy jeeps from the movie, right?"

"Yeah," Toni answers, taking another sip of his DC Cola, "she did. Used to be my favorite toy. That's how I got my Geep way back when."

2

"Shame it got totaled…"

"You were so devastated when I told you the news. We had some good times in that Geep!"

"Like that one time we went off-roading in it!" Joey says. "I was so baked!"

"It was pretty dangerous…" Toni says.

"Who cares? We lived, didn't we?"

"Yeah, but barely-"

"Minor details-"

"I wouldn't call the fact that we got stuck in mud while surrounded by a pack of wild coyotes a 'minor detail'!"

"The tow truck dude came and eventually got us out. So, at the end of the day, does it really matter?"

"The coyote ate my shoe…" Toni sighs.

"There was no physical harm, right?" Joey asks.

"I have a scar on my heel…"

"Okay, so maybe it was dangerous…"

CHAPTER TWO

Toni and Joey are walking from the Outcline, the famous dining hall of Zyuquesne University. The path their feet lays on is known as the B-Walk, made of bright blue bricks the forefathers cast upon the ground one hundred fifty years ago.

Toni has a grin on his face, looking more dazed than a squirrel going nuts.

"Okay..." Joey starts, "what's going on with you, dude?"

"What do you mean?" Toni asks. He looks up at the sky, staring at the clouds that reside in it.

"Something must be on your mind." Joey continues. "You look so... happy now, it's strange."

Toni stops walking, and turns to Joey, who also ends his pace. "Okay, okay. You're right. There is something on my mind."

"Come on, Toni. Spill the beans! You know you can tell me anything."

"It's a bit personal, so I need you to keep this on the down-low."

"Keep what on the 'down-low'?"

"I-I like this girl and--"

"You got a crush on somebody?!" Joey blurts.

"Hey!" Toni shouts. "I told you to keep this on the down-low!" Toni puts his hands in the pockets of his hoodie, clad with a

4

Zyuquesne logo.

"Hi, Toni!" a girl says to him, interrupting their conversation. She's beautiful, with long, brown hair rivaling the length of a sparkling river. "Joey..." she says as she glares at him.

"Hi, Michelle." Toni replies back. "How was that philosophy class?"

"It was boring! Teacher put the whole class to sleep." Michelle checks the time on her phone. It says "12:55." "I gotta head to class. It was nice seeing you, Toni. Bye!" Michelle runs off, waving back at Toni, smiling. Toni waves and smiles back at her.

"Did you know who you were talking to?" Joey asks Toni.

"Um, yeah," Toni replies. "I just talked to Michelle."

"This isn't just any 'Michelle,' dude. It's Michelle Han, one of the finest girls on this campus! You should ask her out."

"I'd love to, but Michelle and I are just friends, nothing more." Toni and Joe start walking again.

"Okay, whatever you say, hotshot..." Joey mumbles.

"Anyway," Toni continues, "I-I like this girl, and... I don't know what to do..."

"Well you've come to the right guy!" Joey exclaims as he puts his arm over Toni's shoulders. "Oh, uh, is she pretty?"

"Why does that matter?!"

"Just asking, that's all!"

"There's more to her than just looks," Toni exclaims.

5

"She's really smart, funny, and she knows the difference between 'your' and 'you're!'"

"Yo, that's amazing!" says a somewhat impressed Joey.

"I'm thinking about reading a poem to her," Toni says.

"Dude, you don't want her to fall in love with a piece of paper!"

"Then what am I supposed to do?" Toni asks as he clutches his chin with his right hand. "You know poetry's my style."

"Well, the first thing you gotta do is get her name. Next, you gotta find out her major. Third, find out where's she from. You wouldn't wanna date somebody that's from, like, West Patricia. That state is really red!"

"Good point," Toni says, "but it isn't Orientation Week, man."

"Those are just the basics, Toni. Last, but not least, the most important part to this puzzle, yo: compliment her and get those digits!"

"That's it? No way..."

"Yes way, my friend! All you gotta do is be yourself, and, sooner or later, somebody will actually wanna go out with you. I remember when I first got to Zyuquesne. All those girls went wild, had helluva time! I fertilized so many gardens and—"

"I get it!" Toni interrupts. "You told this story like a thousand times, dude..."

"My bad," Joey says. "Well, if that girl is what you described, then good luck to ya, my man!"

"Thanks." Toni says as he checks his watch. It says "1:00 PM" on it. "Crap, I'm gonna be late for class!" Toni starts sprinting off to his next class, which is at Prayer Hall, that dingy building on the wrong side of the tracks. "Gotta go! See ya later!"

"Hey, what's her name!?" Joey screams as Toni flees.

Little did Joey know, the girl that's on Toni's mind goes by the name of Reagan Osborne, who is, in fact, all of the attributes that he described to him. Is it possible: can Toni "fertile the garden" that Joey describes with such conviction? The story continues!

CHAPTER THREE

Michelle is inside Czarbucks, a coffee shop that resides on Zyuquesne's campus. It is the host of very mediocre coffee, relatively stale cookies, and souvenir cups that cost five hundred dollars. Inside is what you'd expect from a coffee shop: plenty of tables, chairs, decent lighting, and, last but not least, baristas that look like their souls have been sucked away by the grueling parasite that is called life.

"What's taking her so long?" Michelle asks, twiddling her fingers in frustration. "How can you be late for a meeting that you set up? Typical of her to do that…" She crosses her arms, slowly growing impatient with her tardy friend.

A tall, fair-skinned girl walks into Czarbucks, heading for Michelle's table. She has green hair curlier than the fries at the Outcline, eyes as stunning as a diamond ring, lips juicier than the ripest of fruits, and, above all else, curves that'll make a man go "Dayum, she's finer than a dude getting a speeding ticket!"

The young lady finally shows up to Michelle's table, holding two cups of coffee, taking a seat across from her. "Hey, Michelle!" She hands Michelle a cup.

"Hey, girl, hey!" Michelle excitedly says.

"Ha ha, what's up," Reagan says. "You really need to stop saying that…"

8

"I'm just trying to bring it back, FOREAL, just you wait, Reagan!" Michelle takes sip of her coffee.

"Whatever," Reagan sighs. "OH! I gotta tell you about the guy I've been talking to!"

"I have to tell you about my guy, too—"

"*You* have someone you're talking to?" Reagan slyly asks.

"Chill," Michelle says, "I mean, we haven't spoken to each other yet, okay? Anyway, dude is super cute."

"I thought I was supposed to talk about my guy...?"

"Listen," Michelle starts, "You always got someone you're talking to. When do I ever honestly have a chance?"

"Okay... that's a good point," Reagan replies, "about you barely ever having a chance, not that comment about me... But I do have high hopes with this guy, believe me!"

"Right..." Michelle says as she rolls her eyes. "Anyway, this dude is super cute! He has good hair, a nice smile, and he holds the door for people. And, y'know, those are just the basics."

"C'mon, tell me more," Reagan says in delight, taking a sip of her Czarbucks Slappachino.

"Girl, his muscles... mmm! Nice arms, y'know?"

"Ooh, that sounds amazing! Okay, go on!"

"And he's smart, and I'm talking, like, almost as smart as me!"

"Oh really?" Reagan inquires.

"Yeah," Michelle says. "He'll raise his hand in class

sometimes and actually get the right answer... FOR CALC! What guy can do that, who also happens to be really attractive, too?"

"Wow, he's a rarity," Reagan says. "Does he have a brother?"

"Dunno... but you got someone, don't you?" Michelle says as she glares at Reagan.

"I was kidding! Come on, keep going!"

"Alright, so he's, like, five-ten, and he lives in the Gowers dorm on the twelfth floor. His roommate happens to be Joey... You know him, right?"

"Someone's a bit of a stalker, but, yeah, Joey! That's the bestie! I think I know the guy you're talking about."

"Hmm, maybe..." Michelle sighs. "I gotta go to this poetry club meeting. You know PJ, always long-winded, so this may take a while."

"He's in that club, too?" Reagan asks.

"Didn't he tell you that?"

"No, he didn't. I thought he was only in the choir."

"Maybe if you came to the campus events, you'd know..." Michelle says.

"Okay, okay," Reagan replies, "you should hurry to that poetry club thingy..."

CHAPTER FOUR

Michelle treks up the stairs of Zyuquesne's Student Union, clad with many posters on the walls near the doors, one of which is advertising the Christmas Ball, an event that is two months away. Due to the elevators being on vacation, she continues to climb up the twelve flights of stairs, slowly, but surely getting tired from the ordeal. She eventually reaches the twelfth floor of the Union, making her way to room 1205, where the Poetry Club meeting is being held. Michelle hears a poem being recited in the classroom.

"Maybe it's true," Toni solemnly says, "I am destined to be in the 'friend zone'... forever."

The Poetry Club, all fifteen in unison, snap their fingers, applauding his performance.

"That was beautiful," Essence Wiscrell says, wiping a tear.

"That was dope!" Savannah Almonds says as she wiped her tears off.

"How do you do it?" Megan Boomer asks.

"Runs in the family," Toni replies, chuckling.

"Good job!"

"Thanks." Toni walks back to his seat.

"Sorry, I'm late," Michelle says to Essence as she walks into the room. "Elevator was broken..."

"What a bummer, you missed out on some great stuff," Essence says to Michelle.

Michelle struts to the table parallel to the podium, seeing an empty chair next to where Toni's sitting at. "Hi, Toni," she says to him as she takes a seat next to him in the chair. "Sorry for missing the meeting..."

"It's okay," Toni reassures to Michelle. "Don't worry about it."

"Okay, guys," Essence starts, "this meeting is officially adjou--"

"ANTONIO LANHON!" a voice screams from the back of the room. A tall man with brown dreadlocks comes from the shadows of room 1205, wearing a Duderanger t-shirt and black jeans.

"Paul Edward Summers, Jr," Toni says to him.

"Antonio Lanhon," Paul says, "I would like to be referred to as "PJ," but, more importantly, I have a score to settle with you."

"What score, PJ?"

"Time and time again, you've gotten the admiration from the Poetry Club, while I received nothing but scorn and ridicule. It's time to change that!"

"I didn't realize you took poetry so seriously, but show me what you've got!" Toni proceeds to face-palm in embarrassment.

"This poem is going to blow you all away!" PJ exclaims

to everyone in the room. "I guarantee it, y'all!"

Essence, Savannah, and Megan take their seats, eager to see if PJ can back up his boisterous claims.

"This poem is called 'Workaholic,'" PJ says, "written by yours truly! This poem is even better than the corny stuff you write, Antonio!" PJ aims his pointer finger directly at Toni. "I hope you all enjoy it."

"I guess the meeting isn't over yet," Essence sighs.

"This better be dope," Savannah says.

"Ah-hem!" PJ croaks, clearing his throat. "There was once a man named Marc Armadillo, who had talent that was immeasurable."

One-by-one, the members of the Poetry Club start to fall asleep, not content with the droning voice that PJ has. He sounds as if a robot smoked a joint.

Five thousand lines and twenty minutes later, PJ says, "Unknown to them, he knocked on Heaven's door...," concluding the epic tale he had to share. "Thank you."

Many bodies are slumped over the tables of room 1205, snoozing like a bear in hibernation, but there was one person, who, surprisingly, snapped his fingers, though it was very faint.

"Um..." Essence yawns, "that was good..."

"That... was not dope..." Savannah bluntly says as she stretches her arms.

"Okay, let's take a vote," Megan says. "Raise your hands if you thought Toni was better."

13

All but one person in the classroom raised their hands in favor of Toni.

"Okay, now raise your hands if you thought PJ was better."

Only one person slowly raised his hand in favor of PJ.

"Well, that settles it," Megan says. "The winner of this sudden challenge is Toni! Congrats!"

"You were dope," Savannah says to Toni as she gives him a high five.

"Well done," Essence says to Toni.

"This isn't over, Toni!" PJ shouts. "One day, I'll beat you!" PJ proceeds to storm out of the room like a toddler not getting the toy he wanted on Christmas.

"This meeting is officially adjourned," Essence says. Everyone starts to leave the room, one by one. Toni heads for the door with a smile on his face.

"Hey, Toni," Michelle says, stopping Toni dead in his tracks, "got a minute?"

"Yeah, sure," Toni replies. "So, what's on your mind?" Toni and Michelle start walking down the hallway together.

"Sorry for missing out on your poem..."

"It's no big deal! I can read it to you later if you want."

"R-really," Michelle asks as her face becomes redder than a tomato.

"Yeah," Toni says. "In fact, the one I read wasn't even my

best! Oh, by the way, what's up with you and Joey?"

"What do you mean?"

"Earlier, you looked pissed when you saw him! Did he do something wrong?"

"Um, it's a long story, Toni..." Michelle starts. "Remember the Christmas Ball last year?"

"Uh-huh," Toni replies, "I remember seeing that Ronald Jump guy getting pelted with snowballs outside. Kinda deserved it!"

"Okay, I know that, but something even worse than that happened!"

"Which would be...?"

"You and Joey are pretty tight, no?"

"Yeah, he's my best friend."

"So, at the Christmas Ball, I was sitting at a table with my friends, when suddenly, Joey walks over to us and he asked to dance with me."

"And then what?" Toni asks.

"It was a slow jam, so I took up his 'friendly' offer." Michelle continues. "At first, things were going pretty well. I was having a nice time dancing with him. But then he did the unthinkable: he touched my butt!"

"WHAT?!" Toni's pace screeches to a halt.

"Yes, you heard that right! He put his dirty paws on my derriere, Toni!"

"How could he do that?! I thought he was better than that!"

"Such a heinous action couldn't go unpunished, so I slapped him."

"That explains why his face was so red..." Toni deduces, with his hand clutching his chin.

"That night was embarrassing!" Michelle says. "I can't forgive him for ruining the Christmas Ball for me, in my Freshman year, no less."

"Michelle, that was almost a year ago. I think it's time to move forward from that. Why not bury the hatchet with him?"

"He'll have to apologize first. I should have known better than to dance with him... such a womanizer!"

"Well, I hope you two can clear the air," Toni says optimistically.

"Me, too," Michelle says. "Maybe you're right, I should bury the hatchet." Toni and Michelle continue their stroll down the dimly lit hall. "Oh, yeah, um, what was that poem about?"

"It was about a guy that has bad luck with love."

"Sounds a lot like you, Toni!"

"That's not true!" Toni rubs his nose with his index finger.

"Is there somebody on your mind, lover boy?" Michelle mockingly says to Toni, laughing in the process.

"Yeah," Toni sighs as his face reddens. "Caught me red-handed..."

16

"What's her name?"

"You know Reagan Osborne?"

"Yeah, she's my roommate." Michelle's eyes widen as she quickly finds out who Toni likes. "Oh my gosh!"

"W-what?"

"You got a crush on her?! Well, how come?"

"Well, uh, she's pretty smart, gorgeous, and she knows the difference between their and they're!"

"Really, that's it, Toni? There's more to it, isn't there?"

"I think she's pretty cool," Toni says. "I-I dunno, she just... she rocks my world..."

"If you like her so much, then ask her out," Michelle replies.

"Asking somebody out is not simple, Michelle. It takes a lot of courage and such! Truth be told, I'm scared to death!"

"Come on, Toni, you're better than that! I mean, if you can recite your poetry in front of an audience, then surely you can use that to muster up the courage to ask a girl out!"

"I have an idea: I'll read a poem to Reagan!"

"That's kinda clever, but avoid those clichés, man."

"Ya know," Toni starts, "this pep talk sure came in handy. Thanks, Michelle!" Toni leaves the hall, taking the stairs.

"No problem, Toni," Michelle replies. "Good luck with asking Reagan out!"

CHAPTER FIVE

Later that day, in the evening's embrace, Toni contemplates his plan to win Reagan's heart.

"You don't want her to fall in love with a piece of paper," a thought that has lingered in Toni's mind since his conversation with Joey. "He has a point," Toni says, sitting at his desk, with a pen and paper resting nearby. *"I mean, if you can recite your poetry in front of an audience, then surely you can use that to muster up the courage to ask a girl out,"* another thought that popped up inside his head, reminiscing his talk with Michelle. "Poetry is my passion," Toni states. "I-I don't know what to do!" He grabs his head in frustration, feeling his veins throb against the palms of his hands. "Maybe there's a way I can take both of their suggestions into consideration. I've got it! I can ask Reagan out and recite a poem to her! That ought to work, right?" Toni starts to scribble on his paper, writing what could potentially be a masterpiece among literature.

The next day, Toni sits on a bench on B-Walk, finishing the final draft of his poem. Two people, a blond man and a green-haired woman, walk past him, holding hands. Toni looks up, seeing the couple, and his eyes widen like a sinkhole in a ghost town. "I-Is that Joey and Reagan?!" Toni says to himself in utter disbelief. "I didn't think they'd know each other... oh my god!" He balds up the paper, aware that his plan has backfired.

Toni elects to walk towards Joey and Reagan, yearning to clear the air. He slowly, but steadily struts to them on the blue bricks of B-Walk.

"Hey, Joey" Toni shouts, "what's goin' on?"

"Oh, hey Toni," Joey replies. "I've been meaning to tell you, man. This is Reagan!"

"I know who she is. Hello, Reagan." Toni waves at her. "I mean, are you two together?"

"Yeah!" Reagan exclaims. "Way back when, we met in Chem at the start of the semester, and we hit it off right away."

"I would have told you about us sooner," Joey, as he places his arm over Reagan's shoulders, continues, "but we were trying to keep our relationship on the hush until we were sure we were going to work out."

"That's right," Reagan says, bring her arm around Joey's waist. "Today's the first day we're going public, and I couldn't be happier with that decision!"

"Me neither," Joey says in agreement.

"W-well I'm happy for you guys, too," Toni says, with a vibe of reluctance in his voice. His hands start to shake like a pair of maracas, and his legs buckle like a Jenga tower. "Hey, I'll see ya later," he continues, regaining his composure. "I've got something to do."

"Are you gonna finally ask that girl out?" Joey asks. "I mean, you've talked about her a lot!"

19

"Oh, her? No way, dude. That's all in the past. Where have you been?" Toni chuckles. "She's out of the question now."

"Why, how come?" Reagan asks.

"I just found out she's been taken."

"What a bummer," Joey says in disappointment. "But, hey, look on the bright side: there's plenty of fish in the sea!"

"You're right," Toni replies. "Well, see ya later!" Toni walks away, heading for Gowers.

"See ya!" Joey and Reagan shout in unison.

"*Damn, Joey and Reagan hooked up! But, can I truly be mad at him?*" Toni says in his inner thoughts. "*I should be happy for him, yet I feel like a wild stampede! I gotta be strong, not just for me, but for Joey and Reagan, too!*"

CHAPTER SIX

Later that day, the sun starts to sink low in the sky, preparing for the evening's embrace. Toni, still somewhat shaken up by the revelation earlier, resides at a bench in front of Cottage Hall, near the garden. His face expresses a pain he's never felt before until now: heartbreak.

"What a bummer," Toni murmurs. "It looks like I missed the boat." Toni's head slumps over as he folds his hands. In the corner of his eye, Michelle is heading towards Gowers, clad in her Alpha Beta Cruton cardigan and a navy blue skirt. She notices Toni at the bench, and heads to him.

"Did it not work out?" Michelle asks.

"Huh?! Did what not work out?" Toni replies, completely dazed.

"Snap out of it! C'mon, tell me what happened between you and Reagan, Toni."

"No... it didn't work out," Toni sighs. "Not even a little, and it never does! I don't even know why I'm surprised..."

"Maybe it would help to talk about it," Michelle suggests as she sits next to Toni.

"I want to," Toni replies, "but I'm not sure if I'm ready. Were you heading to class? I don't wanna hold you up."

"Yeah, I was," Michelle answers as she checks the time on

her phone, "but my day isn't exactly going great either. I might cut myself a break. Are you hungry?"

"A little. What's wrong with your day?"

"Hey, I asked you first! But, I guess I'll tell you. Let's walk and talk." Toni and Michelle get up and they stroll down the B-Walk.

"So, I found out today that the guy I like is taken," Michelle starts. "Not only that, but he's with a senior!"

"What's his name?" Toni asks.

"That doesn't matt--"

"Michelle, what's *his* name? This is important!"

"Oh, all right!" Michelle says more annoyed than a comedian getting heckled. "His name is... Jackson Butts."

"Jackson... Butts?" Toni says as a smirk grows on his face. "You've got to be kidding me."

"What're you talking about, Toni? I'm trying to vent to you."

"With a name like that, I don't see how!"

"Toni...!"

"Okay, okay. I'm sorry to hear that. That guy's missing out on something special!"

"So, I guess we're in the same boat then?" Michelle asks.

"Exactly," Toni starts. He gestures his hands frantically. "Far, far out in the middle of the ocean. No sign of land. A coming storm! Monster waves moving fast in our direction!"

22

"Ha ha! You are so dramatic," Michelle says. "I should have figured that since you're a poet."

"Only sometimes!" Toni chuckles.

Toni and Michelle head back to Zyquesne Gowers, and the moon peeks out of the dark sky.

"I never get the girl."

"I never get the guy." Michelle smiles at Toni, with her eyes beaming towards his. Toni also smiles back, but his cheeks become redder than a ketchup bottle. "Um, good night?"

"Yeah, uh, good night, Michelle. I'll see ya tomorrow!"

The two awkwardly head inside Gowers, with Toni going to Gower C, and Michelle going to Gower B. Well, wasn't that an eventful turn of events or what?!

CHAPTER SEVEN

It's almost midnight at Zyquesne University. The B-Walk is empty, with the lights shining on the bricks that lead to the path of success. After a few hours of writing a paper at Funberg Library, Toni heads back to Gowers to get some rest. However, something else pops up in his mind.

"*I should clear up the air with Joey,*" Toni thinks to himself. "*This whole situation regarding Reagan will be even more awkward if I don't tell him about it.*" He heads up to his room on the fifth floor of Gower C. On the scratched up door, it reads a number: "505." Toni goes into the room and sees Joey in his bed watching a movie on his laptop, while eating a bag of chips. Joey glances at Toni, and he takes off his earbuds.

"Hey, Toni," Joey says to him. "How's that paper comin' along?"

"Never mind the paper," Toni replies, "I need to talk to you about something. It's important."

"Fire away."

"I never told you about the girl I liked, right?"

"Yeah, I didn't even get a chance to find out the name."

"Well, um," Toni stammers, "the girl that I had a crush on... was Reagan Osborne."

"What?!" Joey gasps. "I can't believe what I just heard!"

"Yeah, it's surprising..."

"Why didn't you tell me this sooner?!"

"Based on your reaction, I didn't want to give you a heart attack."

"Toni, I would've helped you get with her. You know that, man. I mean, when you saw Reagan and I together, you didn't look so good..."

"I was crushed," Toni says, "but I realized that I can't be mad that you're with her. I'm happy for you two! I'm sorry that I went up to you like that earlier. It was rude."

"Forget about it," Joey says. "I forgive you. I'm glad you told me this, Toni. I appreciate your honesty."

"Thanks." A smile emerges onto Toni's face.

CHAPTER EIGHT

$\mathbf{A}$ new day approaches Zyuquesne University. The squirrels makes the gardens of the campus their playground. Reagan is at the library, printing out her essay on why "Chocolate is a Drug." She feels her phone vibrate in her back pocket, receiving a text from Michelle saying, "Meet me at the DaeSpot at the union. It's urgent!" Reagan quickly grabs her stuff and heads over there.

"I'm glad you read my message," Michelle says as Reagan takes a seat inside the DaeSpot.

"You did say it was 'urgent,'" Reagan replies, "So, what's up?"

"Keep this between you and me, okay?"

"You know it, girl!"

"So, you know about that cute guy I mentioned, like, a month ago?"

"Yeah, what about him?" Reagan asks.

"His name is Toni," Michelle confesses.

"Toni? You mean that poet guy, right?"

"Yeah, he's the one." Michelle places her hands on her heart. "I really like him and… I don't know how to tell him."

"I've been in your footsteps before." Reagan tells Michelle. "I was anxious when I first asked Joey out. But, the one

26

thing that saved me from disaster was confidence. Girl, you gotta believe in yourself!"

"I know that. It's just that Toni and I have been friends for years. I never really thought that I could be more than just his friend till now."

"Oh, I see. I mean, what made you develop those feelings for him?"

"Well," Michelle starts, "whenever I see him write, he looks so passionate. I appreciate that. Toni's such a sweet guy. Smart, kind, and handsome – the things I like in a guy. He has those traits and then some!

"Wow, you *really* like him, don't you?" Reagan asks.

"Y-yes…" Michelle stutters. Her cheeks become as red as an apple.

"I think you should ask him out."

"That's been on my mind for a while, but I'm broke."

"Well, maybe I can fix that!" Reagan says. She pulls a twenty-dollar bill out her pocket. "Here, take this."

"I can't just take your money like that!" Michelle yelps. "I gotta pay you back!"

"Don't worry about. Just have a good time!"

"Thanks, Reagan! You're the best!"

"Anything for my friend. So, what're you gonna wear?"

"I haven't decided that nor asked him out…" Michelle sighs….

"We're gonna plan ahead for this," Reagan declares. "To the clothing store!"

After a long bus ride on the highway to Heaven, Reagan and Michelle arrive at the clothing store known as EJ Faxx. They step inside and there's a whole array of clothing, for both men and women.

"It's like stepping into a candy store!" Michelle says excitedly. "Why didn't you tell me about this place?"

"I dunno," Reagan replies, "you never asked, I never got a chance. So much has been happening, y'know?"

"Regardless, this place looks neat!" Michelle points to the dresses section. "Let's go over there!"

"Okay, pick a few things and try 'em on."

Michelle grabs a flower-patterned dress and sprints over to the dressing room like an ex-con escaping prison.

"So," Michelle says as she steps out of the dressing room wearing the dress. "What do you think?"

"Damn, girl!" Reagan says. "You look foine!"

Michelle looks in the mirror, checking herself out. She notices something perplexing.

"Does this dress make my butt look big?" Michelle asks.

"Nothin' wrong with a little junk in the trunk," Reagan assures. "You look great."

"Thanks. Now that I think about it, I love these curves!"

"That's the spirit, girl! I think our work is done here."

CHAPTER NINE

"Toni, take the shot," Joey yells. "We ain't got all day!"

"Alright, alright," Toni replies. He shoots the basketball, and he misses the hoop. The ball bounces into the weight room.

"Aw man… You were so close!"

"Well, I did warn you that I was rusty, didn't I?" Toni wipes the sweat off his face with his towel. He and Joey both head into the locker room.

"You really gotta work on those foul shots, man." Joey snarks at Toni.

"At least I can make a lay-up, unlike a certain somebody," Toni snarks back at Joey, giving him a side-glance.

"Touché. So, how's everything between you and your girlfriend?"

"Girlfriend? What girlfriend, Joey?"

"Michelle, duh!"

"She's not my girlfriend!" Toni yells. "I already told you we're just friends."

"Well, judging by the way she acts around you, she wants to be more than just a friend, Toni," Joey replies.

"What do you mean?"

"Last week, the way Michelle said 'hi' to you. Compare that to the way she said my name. It's like she's mad at me or somethin'…"

"She *is* mad at you."

"For what?!" Joey asks. "I haven't done anything to her recently."

"That's the thing!" Toni exclaims. "It's not because of recent events. You were at the Christmas Ball last year, right?"

"Yeah, so?"

"Michelle's still pissed at you for touching her butt while dancing with her. She wants an apology."

"That slap she gave me was well deserved. I feel pretty bad for doing that to her. This apology's long overdue!"

"Thanks, Joey."

"No problem. Um, you are gonna ask her out, right?"

"I've been thinking about it," Toni claims. "But, I think it'll be a little awkward…"

"It won't awkward," Joey says. "Remember: just be yourself. Go text her, dude!"

Toni takes out his phone and he texts "Hi, Michelle. Would you like to go out with me?" After a minute of contemplation, he doesn't press "send" on his phone. Instead, he erases the message! "No, I won't text her. I'll ask her in person!"

"Whoa, pretty gutsy move if you try that! Good luck."

"Thanks. I just hope I can keep my composure." Toni whips out his phone, sending this message to Michelle: "Hi, can you meet me at the Gowers lobby?"

"Sure. What for?" Michelle's reply read.

"It's a surprise," Toni texts back. "Meet me in one hour."

"OK. Bye." Michelle responds.

"Welp, it's time to get this inquiry off my chest!" Toni says. "I better hurry over there before it's too late."

"Me too," Joey says. "I'm gonna apologize to her before you do your thang."

"Let's get moving!" Toni and Joey change out of their basketball gear and headed for Gowers.

Meanwhile, on the other side of the campus, Michelle arrives to Gowers ten minutes early.

"*I wonder what Toni's up to,*" Michelle thinks to herself. "*Is he gonna do what I think he's gonna do? Is this one of Joey's pranks?*" She sits in the lobby, eagerly anticipating Toni.

"Wow, she beat us to the punch already!" Toni says as he and Joey walk to Gowers.

"She's waitin' for ya," Joey says.

Toni and Joey walk inside of the Gowers lobby, seeing Michelle sitting at one of the couches. They head over to her.

"Hi, Toni!" Michelle squees.

"Hi, Michelle," Toni replies.

"What do you want, Joey?" Michelle says sternly.

"I want to apologize," Joey starts, "for what I did to you at the Christmas Ball last year. It was bad and inexcusable. I didn't mean to ruin your night like that. I'm sorry."

"I…" Michelle opens with reluctance, "forgive you." She puts her hand out.

Joey shakes her hand and says, "Thank you." He "checks" the time on his phone. "Well, that was great and all, but I gotta go! Bye!" Joey immediately leaves Gowers, going as fast as a mouse whenever it spots cheese.

"So, Toni, you wanted to meet me here for something?" Michelle asks.

"Yeah," Toni starts. "This was important so I have to ask you in person!"

"What's on your mind?"

"Um, well, I... uh... do you... wanna catch... a movie sometime...?"

"Yeah, I'd love to! What're we seeing?"

"*Sunlight*. Is Friday night okay?"

"No, got a ZPC night to attend," Michelle replies, "but Saturday's good."

"Cool." Toni says. "So, I'll see you on Saturday?"

"Yep. I can't wait to see *Sunlight*! Bye, Toni!" Michelle goes back to Gower B with a grin on her face.

"Bye!" Toni says to Michelle happily. He goes outside, jumping in excitement. "I did it! I'm going out on date, and who better than one of my closest friends?"

"She said 'yes'?!" Joey asks as he emerges from a trashcan with a banana peel on his head, while hold a pair of binoculars.

"Yup. We're gonna see *Sunlight* on Saturday."

"*Sunlight*? Seen it!" Joey sees Toni glare at him, looking more furious than a bull seeing red. "But, a good choice either way…"

CHAPTER TEN

"So, how'd it go," Reagan asks Michelle. They're back in their room at Gowers B, number 843. The moonlight shines on their window like a singer's octaves at a talent show.

"I think it went pretty well," Michelle replies.

"Did you ask him out?"

"Even better. *He* asked me out!"

"Oh my gosh, this is amazing!" Reagan screams as she hops up and down like a bunny. "You did say 'yes,' right?"

"Of course!" Michelle says, as she jumps around like a frog. "We're gonna see *Sunlight* on Saturday."

"Wow, that's a great choice. Be wary of that scene with the gyne—"

"Hey! Don't spoil the movie for me!"

"My bad." Reagan says. "I hope you two have a great time. Will you kiss him?"

"What?!" Michelle gasps. "It's only the first date, Reagan! I think it's a little soon to just start making out like that…"

"Sorry, I keep getting ahead of myself. Look, just keep your cool, and… have fun."

"Thanks. Good night."

"Good night, lover girl!"

Three days have passed since the immortal question was

asked. Thus, the main event is about to go underway! What is this "main event," you ask. Well, it's… a date. A date of destiny, where one's dreams can potentially come true! Wait, never mind what I just said. Anyway, Toni and Michelle start to get ready for their night out.

Toni is at Gower C, getting ready for the date. The hairs on his arms start to stand up like kids reciting the Pledge of Allegiance. *"I feel so anxious!"* Toni thinks to himself. *"I gotta stay calm and just… go with the flow."*

"Lookin' sharp," Joey says as he sees Toni, who is wearing a navy blue sweater, jeans, and a black leather jacket.

"Thanks," Toni says. "I'll see ya later!" He leaves room 505, heading for the lobby.

Back at Gower B, room 843, Michelle is ready to go out on the date. *"As Reagan said, just 'keep your cool and have fun.'"* Michelle thought to herself. *"This night's gonna be something else…"*

"You look beautiful," Reagan says to Michelle. She stretches her arms out, signaling for a hug.

"Thanks, Reagan," Michelle replies. She and Reagan hug each other. Michelle heads for the door.

"Have fun." Reagan glances at a jacket and throws it to Michelle. "Oh, and don't forget your jacket!"

"Thanks. See you later!" Michelle struts for the lobby, where Toni is waiting at.

"W-Wow." Toni says in awe. "You look gorgeous!"

Michelle's dress hugs the curves of her body, with a flower pattern caressing the hot pink cloth of it. She's also wearing a light blue denim jacket, and her smile is as bright as the sun on a hot, summer day.

"Thank you," Michelle says in delight. "Ready to go?"

"Yeah." Toni replies. "Um, how are we gonna get there?"

"My car."

"You have a car?! I'm kinda jealous…" Toni and Michelle walk out to the parking lot. They head over to the green Cord Stallion, one of the most popular cars in the world.

"Yeah, my parents got this for my 16th birthday. Let's hop in!" Michelle unlocks the car, and they both strap themselves in. Off to the theater they go!

Ten thousand red lights and fifteen minutes later, the pair arrives to North Side Lurks, the second-largest movie theater in the city of Blitzburgh.

"This place is pretty nice," Toni says.

"Never been here before?" Michelle asks as they both go to the concession stand.

"First time. I usually went to Fireworks Cinema for movies." Toni's eyes gaze at the prices of the snacks and food. They widen like a balloon upon this revelation: "Ten dollars for a box of candy?! Are they out of their mind?!"

"I knew you'd freak out at those prices. I have an idea!"

36

Michelle grabs Toni by the wrist, leading him out of the theater.

"Where are we going?"

"You'll see!" Michelle takes Toni to a nearby store called "Socket Whiz," which sells candy and drinks at a much more reasonable price.

"Whoa!" Toni yells. "This place has everything. High quality stuff at a cheap price? Count me in!" He grabs three boxes of candy and two bottles of soda, one apple pie flavored, and the other chocolate flavored. Michelle takes one Wrestlee Bar and a Diet Woke.

"Your total is $9.99," says the cashier wearing a wig as yellow as a banana.

"Thanks," Toni says as he hands the cashier a ten-dollar bill. "Keep the penny." They place the junk in Michelle's purse.

"Isn't that place awesome?!" Michelle boasts as they head over to Theater 9, where the movie will be played.

"I gotta go there more often," Toni replies with joy. They take their seats in Theater 9 and the movie *Sunlight* starts to play.

Two empty bottles of soda and thirty minutes later, Toni and Michelle are enjoying the movie. However, something pops up in the former's mind.

"*The movie's great and all*," Toni starts in the recluse of his mind, "*but I gotta make a move! A-ha! I've got it!*" He stretches his arms out and places one over Michelle's shoulders.

"*Oh my, his arm's over me*," Michelle thinks, noticing his gesture, blushing in the process.

As the movie progressed, Michelle starts leaning towards Toni, and he starts to blush as he sees her, so he leans towards her.

"*This is it,*" Michelle thinks. "*My first kiss…*" She closes her eyes…

"*Is this really happening,*" Toni asks himself deep down. "*Am I gonna seal the deal?*" He shuts the doors on his set of eyes.

Michelle and Toni move closer and closer towards each other like magnets seeing a refrigerator. Unfortunately for them, the light's come on, and the movie's over. They both back away from one another, reddening in embarrassment.

After a somewhat awkward car ride back to Zyuquesne, they return to Gowers, arriving in the lobby.

"Well, I had a great time," Michelle says.

"Yeah, me too," Toni replies.

"I'd love to go out again sometime." The two smile and hug each other. "Good night."

"Good night," Toni says to Michelle as she heads back to Gower B. Thus, the date between these characters has concluded. What will happen next time? Stay tuned!

CHAPTER ELEVEN

Morning approaches Zyuquesne University, where the birds are chirping and where the leaves take their leaps of faith off the branches from whence they came. Toni is inside the Rogan Dining Hall, home to the finest pizza that the average college student puts up with. He takes a sip of his glass of Mountain Krew soda.

"Last night sure was amazing," Toni mutters to himself. He sees Reagan walking towards his table, wearing a Zyuquesne sweater and black leggings, a surprisingly common attire on the campus during this time of year. She parks her caboose at the table.

"Hey, Toni," Reagan says to him. "Got a minute?"

"Sure," Toni replies. "Need anything?"

"I know we haven't talked to each other often, but I gotta ask you something: how was your date with Michelle?"

"I had a great time!" His face starts to light up like a Christmas tree. "The movie was great and she took me to this really cool store with all sorts of candy and dri-"

"Besides all of that," Reagan interrupts, "did you... spend 'quality time' with her?"

"I beg your pardon?" Toni asks in confusion.

"I mean, did you two kiss?"

"Well, um..."

"Toni!"

"N-no…"

"Well, there's always next time," Reagan reassures. "Or, at least until you're ready."

"Now, I've got a question for you," Toni claims as he drinks the Mountain Krew. "How'd your first date go?"

"Me? Hmm… Joey and I saw *Sunlight* a few weeks ago."

"Joey told me he saw it. Nearly spoiled the movie for me… what'd you think of it?"

"Um… I know that Sugar Mommy was eatin' out before the feds arrived and… I can't remember…" Reagan adjusts her glasses, struggling to piece together what happened in the movie.

"You didn't watch the movie, did you?" Toni asks.

"You got me," Reagan replies. "Joey and I made out through the whole thing…"

"I'm shocked! Off all movies to kiss during, you chose *Sunlight*?!"

"To be honest, we were kinda bored, and we just… got in the mood. At least you and Michelle liked it. So, you're gonna go out with her again, right?"

"I'd love to," Toni says. "The second time around won't be so awkward! I just don't know where to go…"

"Try the Fruitcake Factory on the South Side," Reagan suggests. "She's never been there before."

"'Fruitcake Factory'? Sounds interesting. How's their

food?"

"Some of the best fruitcake you can possibly get in the United States of Paprika!"

"That good, huh? Well, now I gotta go there!"

"And you couldn't have found a better person to go with," Reagan says.

"You're right!" Toni replies. "I'll ask her about, and just go from there."

"She's gonna love it!" Reagan gets up from the extra seat at Toni's table. "It was nice talking to you, Toni. You're kinda cool!"

"Right back at'cha! See ya later!"

Later that day, in the brink of the afternoon, Michelle meets up with Reagan for lunch at the Outcline, the place to be if you want overcooked chicken tenders and watery soft drinks.

"Check this out," Reagan starts. "Toni told me he had a great time last night."

"Uh-huh," Michelle replies. "And then what?"

"He told me he wants to go out with you again!"

"Oh my gosh!" Michelle crosses her arms. "Are you lying to me?"

"No, I'm serious! He wants to go to the Fruitcake Factory with you."

"'Fruitcake Factory'? What's the catch?"

"There is no catch," Reagan explains. "Neither you nor

Toni never went there, so it'd be fun if you went to a new place for the first time."

"That's a good point," Michelle replies. "Their food must be good!"

"Speaking of that, let's put those meal swipes to use!"

"You ran out of ZYQ bucks already?!"

"A girl's gotta eat, y'know!"

CHAPTER TWELVE

"**A**lright, we're here," Michelle says to Toni as she parks the car in the lot of the Fruitcake Factory. The exterior of the place is what you would expect from any fancy restaurant: bricks, somewhat clean windows, some doors, and a giant sign. The two step inside this "magical wonderland" of a restaurant. The décor reminds people of those old animated movies from the 1950s. There's also a map of Blitzburgh, Bennsylvania in the heart of the restaurant, also known as "the back."

"This place looks beautiful," Toni says, "but it's not as stunning as you."

"That's sweet," Michelle replies as her cheeks (once again) redden. "Let's find a good seat."

Michelle and Toni go to a table a few clicks north from "the back." Toni pulls out a chair for Michelle.

"Thank you," Michelle says, appreciating the gesture. Toni pushes her in. "First time for everything, huh?"

"Yeah," Toni replies. "It's no fun when you don't try anything new."

"You can say that again! Funny question, but do have any siblings?"

"I have a twin brother."

"You have a twin?!" Michelle asks ecstatically.

"Yeah, he goes to culinary school," Toni replies.   43

"How come I never saw him? Never mentioned him, either… was he hiding?"

"He… usually did his own thing. But, he's pretty cool once you get to know him. I also have an older sister. I think she's coming to visit."

"I can't wait to meet her! Is she finished with school?" Michelle asks.

"She graduated from the Community College of Challageni County a few years back," Toni answers. "Top of her class."

"C4! My brother went there! Unlike your sis, he flunked…"

"How'd that happen?"

"C4 is known for being quite the party school… It's a miracle your sis graduated there."

"I hope he didn't give up," Toni says.

"He didn't," Michelle replies. "He transferred to Yarnegie Mango and got his act together."

"That's wonderful! Yarnegie Mango's one of the top schools in the country."

"Are you ready to order," the waiter asks the two.

"I'll take the Bruiser Bean Special Fruitcake," Michelle tells the waiter.

"Hmm…" Toni starts, "I'll take the, uh… Yinzer Deluxe Fruitcake."

44

"Excellent choice," the waiter tells Toni. "I'll right with you in just a minute." The waiter skips back to the front of the restaurant.

"So, Toni, how come you don't drive?"

"Well... It's a long story..."

"Did it involve Joey?" Michelle snickers.

"Yeah," Toni answers. "Joey and I took my Geep off-road in the deserts of Mollifornia. One thing led to another, and the Geep got destroyed."

"That *really* sucks. Were you stranded?"

"Only for an hour. We hitched a ride in a tow truck. Before that, we were attacked by coyotes!"

"Coyotes?! Like the ones from *The Jaguar Queen*?"

"Yep. Even got a scar on my heel from one of 'em!" Toni feels his phone vibrate in his pocket. "Excuse me." Toni answers the phone. "Hello... what... she's in the hospital?! I-I'm on my way!"

"What's going on?" Michelle asks.

"My sister's in the hospital... I have to go." Toni gets up from his seat, ready to leave.

"I can drive you there."

"Thanks, Michelle." Toni and Michelle head straight for the hospital.

"Hey, you forgot to tip!" The waiter yells as he sees them leave the Fruitcake Factory.

"How is she, doctor?!" Toni frantically asks the doctor at the hospital.

"Your sister Deborah is in fair condition, young man," the doctor answers calmly. "It's a miracle she had her seat belt on."

"Thanks, doctor."

"She's sleeping now, but you can see her if you want." The doctor heads back into another patient's room.

"I'm glad she's okay," Michelle says.

"Me, too," Toni replies. "I didn't want to lose her. She means a lot to me."

"Toni," his mother calls. "Deborah got into a car accident. Fell asleep at the wheel…"

"She's still with us," Toni replies. "Thank the lord!"

"Deborah's gonna make a speedy recovery," Toni's dad says, joining the conversation. "I'm glad you made it here, Toni." Toni's dad spots Michelle sitting at a bench in the hall. "Who's that?"

"That's Michelle, Dad. She's a great friend of mine."

Hi, I'm Mr. Lanhon, Toni's father," he says to Michelle as he puts his hand out for a handshake.

"Michelle Han, sir." She shakes Mr. Lanhon's hand.

"So you're that 'Michelle' girl that Toni mentioned?" Toni's mom asks. "I'm Mrs. Lanhon, his mother. It's nice to meet you!"

"Pleasure's all mine."

46

Michelle, Toni and his family all go into Deborah's room. She has bandages over the cuts and bruises sustained during the accident. Her eyes start to open up, with everything being foggier than a morning traffic rush.

"Hey…" Deborah lightly says to everyone in the room, "how's it going?"

"Deborah," Mrs. Lanhon starts, "we're here now, baby."

"I love you…" Deborah has a sigh of relief upon seeing her family.

"We love you, too, Debbie," Mr. Lanhon says. The Lanhon family goes to hug Deborah, coming together like a puzzle.

"Ow! Watch the ribs…" Deborah and the others all start to laugh as they embrace one another.

Two weeks fly by like bees pollenating a garden, and Deborah is able to walk out of the hospital on her own alongside her family.

"You should have Michelle come over for Thanksgiving dinner," Deborah tells Toni as they head to the car.

"That's a good idea," Toni replies. "It would be nice to have a guest over for once."

"Remember when we helped Mom make the cookies?"

"They got burnt because of us! And then you framed me!"

"Good time, Toni. Good times…"

CHAPTER THIRTEEN

"**H**ello," Toni starts, holding the house phone.

"Hello?" Michelle replies from her phone. "What's up?"

"I was wondering if you could come over to my house for Thanksgiving dinner."

"That sounds nice! I'd love to know more about your folks."

"So, I'll see you on Thursday?"

"Marked my calendar. See you soon! Bye."

"Bye." Toni hangs up the phone the way old people hang their laundry. He walks into the kitchen, witnessing Deborah make a strawberry smoothie, putting in the fruit, milk, and you know the rest.

"So, she's coming over?" Deborah asks.

"Yup," Toni answers. "She even marked her calendar."

"*Berry* impressive!"

"Debbie…!" Toni face-palms, attempting to hide his grin.

"My bad… I'm surprised, Toni. I didn't think you'd be quite the ladies' man."

"Me neither. Michelle and I've been dating these past few weeks. She's great."

"I'm glad you've found someone so wonderful." Deborah turns on the blender, creating something tastier than anything below the belt on a Saturday evening. "You kiss her yet?"

"Why does everyone ask that question?" Toni inquires to himself. "N-no…"

"Why not? I mean, you like her, don't you?"

"I'm just waiting for the right time."

"I don't mean to pressure you. Just that my baby bro's got a girlfriend and he's lost."

"I am not lost! Look, I don't wanna talk about it. Let's just move onto something else, okay?!" Toni folds his hands and takes a breath deeper than the average college ethics course.

"Okay," Deborah says. "Whatever you say, kid." Deborah takes a sip of her smoothie, with a texture so rich it can end world hunger.

"I'm sorry." Toni looks Deborah straight in the eye.

"For what?"

"Back in August, after we had dinner at the Pizza Shack, you dropped me off at the school…"

CHAPTER ZERO

"We're back," Deborah said to Toni. The car was in Zyuquesne's parking lot and it was filled to the brim with automobiles.

"Thanks for the ride and pizza, Debbie," Toni said. See ya in a—

"Wait, I have to talk to you."

"What is it now?"

"I just want to tell you that you did a great job last year."

"Thanks. I sure knocked it out of park, didn't I?"

"Here's the thing: it's one thing to be confident, it's another to be arrogant."

"What am I being arrogant about? You saw my grades, right?"

"Toni, bragging about how smart you are is just gonna piss everyone off, including your friends. Believe me, I was once in your footsteps."

"What's with the lecture, Deborah?"

"Lecture? I'm just giving you advice. Now, I know I'm not your real sister—"

"Then stop pretending to be!" Toni's face became an ugly frown. Deborah's eyes widened like a deer in the headlights, shocked by Toni's choice of words. Toni got out of the car.

"Have a nice semester…" Deborah said solemnly to Toni before she drove off. As she drove away, Toni's face expressed disappointment like a child not having candy on Halloween.

CHAPTER THIRTEEN

"Those words still sting," Deborah says to Toni. "I couldn't believe my ears when you said that."

"I regret saying that to you," Toni replies. "It was *way* out of line."

"I forgive you, Toni. Siblings go through so much. But, at

the end of the day, they still have each other's back."

"Thank you." Toni and Deborah hug each other, their sibling bond continuing to go strong.

One week passes by like a man missing the bus on his way to work, and it's Thanksgiving! Michelle rings the doorbell of the Lanhon house, number 1997 in the West End, on the elusive street known as "Ebbert." The door opens up and Mrs. Lanhon appears with a smile on her face.

"Hi, Michelle," Mrs. Lanhon says. "I'm glad you're here, missy, 'cause we're havin' one helluva feast today!"

"Hi, Mrs. Lanhon," Michelle replies. "Is Toni here?" She and Toni's mom walk inside the house, shutting the door behind them.

"Yeah, he's helping with dinner. He's baking an apple pie."

"I see, cooking runs in the family!"

"Mm-hmm! C'mon, have a seat."

Michelle takes a seat at the table in the dining room. The rest of the family follows the matriarch of the household, taking their seats as well.

"Alright, everyone," Mr. Lanhon says, "Join your hands for the prayer." Everyone takes a hand, becoming a circle in unison.

"Thank you, God, for the food. Thank you for your nurturing. And thank you for those we love. Amen," they all say together.

"Alright, let's dig in," Toni says ecstatically. "Could you please pass the sweet potatoes?"

"Sure," Deborah replies, passing the orange potatoes over.

"So, that's Michelle," Michael, Toni's twin, asks, whispering in his ear.

"Yeah," Toni replies.

"She's cute!" Michael stuffs his face with collard greens.

"The food's great, Mr. and Mrs. Lanhon," Michelle says happily.

"Thank you," Mr. Lanhon replies.

"Who wants mac and cheese?!" Mrs. Lanhon asks, beaming with excitement. She eyeballs Toni, who looks more hesitant than a person on a diving board.

"No thanks," Toni says.

"Aw, come on. You used to eat this all the time when you were younger!"

"Well, uh, things changed…"

"It tastes great, Toni," Deborah claims as she eats a forkful of the macaroni and cheese.

"I agree," Michelle says. "It's yummy!"

"I mean if I can eat it," Michael starts, "then so can you, bro!"

"Okay, okay! I'll… try the mac and cheese," Toni says reluctantly. He puts a bit of it on his plate, proceeding to take a forkful, and holding it to his face. "Here goes…"

52

"Yes, you can do it son," Mrs. Lanhon encourages.

Toni eats the forkful of the mac and cheese, chewing it slower than a turtle walking this deteriorating Earth. "Hmm… it's… not bad."

"I-I can't believe my ears," Mr. Lanhon gasps.

"H-he… likes it!" Mrs. Lanhon says.

"So, Toni," Michelle starts, "How come you hated mac and cheese for so long?"

"Well, it's a long story," Toni replies. "I liked it as a kid, then I just… stopped eating it. That's all."

"What a compelling story," Deborah says. "You'll get a Pulitzer!" Everyone at the table laughs at the mediocre joke.

Ten minutes later, it's time for the dishes, AKA, the "most dreadful time to be in the kitchen."

"Toni, it's your turn to do the dishes!" Mrs. Lanhon yells at him.

"Aww man…" Toni sighs. The pile of dishes was the size of a junkyard. "I can't do all this by myself…"

"Fine. Michael, go help your brother with the dishes!"

"What?!" Michael asks in shock. "I did them last year…" He sees his mother glare angrier than a man dressed as a bat. "O-Okay…" Toni and Michael both go to the sink to do the dishes.

"Michelle," Deborah starts. "Can we talk for a moment?"

"Sure," Michelle replies. "What about?" She and Deborah head for the porch, where there's privacy and lightning bugs.

"You're dating my little brother, right?"

"Yeah. He's a sweetheart."

"I just want to thank you for being by his side at the hospital."

"Oh, it's nothing."

"You're a good girl, Michelle. I wish there were more gals like you around!"

"Um, t-thanks…?" Michelle's face becomes as red as the barbeque sauce that was slathered all over the baby back ribs they just had as part of their dinner. "I have a question for you."

"Which would be?" Deborah asks.

"If I want to impress at the Christmas Ball, what should I wear?"

"Kind weird to ask your boyfriend's sister, but wear what feels comfortable. Toni won't even mind if you're wearing a trash bag for a dress!"

"For real?"

"Yeah. Just pick something from your closet and have a good time."

"Thanks for the pep talk. You're a great sister."

"I try my best."

After a tumultuous time washing the dishes and having dessert, Thanksgiving dinner was a success.

"I gotta go," Michelle says to the family.

"It was nice having you, Michelle," Mr. Lanhon says to

her.

"You should bring your family along next year," Mrs. Lanhon suggests.

"Even better: Easter!" Michael says.

"I ask my parents about it," Michelle insists.

"See ya back at school," Toni says to Michelle.

"Bye, Toni." Michelle and Toni hug each other, to the complete and baffling dismay of his family.

"Bye." Toni waves and Michelle does the same as she departs in her car.

CHAPTER FOURTEEN

The Christmas Ball is right around the corner for Zyuquesne University! It's that special time of year for students that want to relax and have fun before the grueling Finals Week kicks into high gear. The sun rises from its grave to deliver upon the sunlight that warms us with hope and despair. Toni returns from his Thanksgiving Break, back at Gowers, aware that the Christmas Ball will be in his court in less than a week.

"I gotta get a suit," Toni says, "and fast! Know any good places?"

"Yeah," Joey answers. "There's this clothing store called 'Subarashii,' and they sell and tailor suits at discounted prices. That's where I got my tux last year."

"Sounds pretty neat, but where's it at?"

"They recently opened a new location in Gloomfield. You should check that one out."

"Cool, so it's a bus ride away from here. Thanks, man!"

"No problem, Toni."

Toni sets forth on his journey to Subarashii. Little did Toni know, rain is on the forecast.

One bus ride and swindled out three dollars later, Toni arrives near the store. To his dismay, it was closed.

"Damn," Toni says. "Should've brought my umbrella…"

To pass the time, he waited across the street from Subarashii, eager to get in before anyone else. The raindrops poured down faster than syrup going through a waffle's maze. Twenty minutes pass by, and the sign on the door changes from "CLOSED" to "OPEN."

"Finally!" Toni steps inside Subarashii, more drenched than a salad with excess dressing.

"How may I help you, sir," one of the clerks asks Toni. She's a short, blonde woman wearing a dark blue-violet suit with white stripes. Her eyes are blue and piercing like nail through a wall.

"Pardon me, do you have any suits in black?"

"Unfortunately, all of the black suits are sold out. So many funerals these days…"

"Okay, got any grey suits?"

"Yes we do. Nothing too tacky, right?" The clerk shows Toni the selection of grey suits present at the store. She picks out the solid medium grey set from the hanger rack. "What do you think of this?"

"Hmm, looks good," Toni replies. "May I try it on?"

"Sure. Take as much time as you need. The changing rooms are in the back."

"Thank you." Toni heads to the changing room, which is more secluded than the new kid at her first day of school.

Five minutes pass and Toni steps out of the changing room wearing the suit.

"I like it," Toni says to the clerk. "How much for it?"

"Sixty dollars," the clerk replies.

"What?! Sixty bucks?!"

"This is cheaper compared to other stores. Either that or nothing, kid."

"Fine, I'll pony up the cash." Toni gives the cashier sixty dollars, and the suit is officially his. He walks out of Subarashii with something nice to wear for the Christmas Ball.

Meanwhile, on the other side of town, back at EJ Faxx, Michelle and Reagan are picking out dresses for the Ball. The former steps out of the changing room wearing a dark green dress.

"Does this dress expose too much shoulder," Michelle says as she adjusts the spaghetti strap.

"Really, Michelle," Reagan asks. "We already went through this arc in Chapter Eight!"

"I'm just kidding! I love this dress! You're looking good." Michelle's eyes pans over Reagan's body like a camera exposing a bank robbery.

"Understatement of the year, girl!" Reagan's wearing a strapless crimson dress that really *pushes* things up! "This Christmas Ball's gonna be great!"

"That'll be two hundred fifty dollars and twenty-five cents," says the cashier. Michelle and Reagan pay for the dresses and they make their way back to Zyuquesne, also prepared for the Christmas Ball.

The five-day interlude between those shopping trips and the Christmas Ball goes quicker than the first time in a room lit with candles, as a classic slow jam plays in the background. The snow falls onto the campus, descending from the dark, grey sky.

"For once, you have something that fits," Joey snarks. "You look like a made man, Toni."

"Thanks," Toni replies. "You don't look too bad yourself. Let's go!"

Toni and Joey leave their room at Gowers, going to the Union, where Michelle and Reagan are waiting at. The shuttle parked in front is what'll take the students to the Christmas Ball, located at the Charity Hotel near Stallion Square.

"Hey, ladies," Joey says to Reagan and Michelle. He gives Reagan a kiss as Michelle hugs Toni.

"Ready to dance, Toni," Reagan asks.

"Well," Toni starts, "it depends on the song…"

"It's okay if you can't dance," Michelle says.

"Excuse me," Toni says. "I'll be right back. Gotta get something to drink."

"Better hurry," Joey replies. "Shuttle's leavin' in five minutes."

"Don't worry, I'll be fast!" Toni quickly heads into the Czarbucks to get a cup of coffee. He immediately heads out, but something catches his eye: a young man trips in the snow, with his books scattered on the ground.   59

"Hey, are you okay?" Toni asks the guy as he walks over to him.

"Yeah, I've had better days…" the guy replies.

"What's your name?"

"Stephen. Stephen Garter."

"I think I've seen you before… you were at Orientation, right?" Toni wipes the snow off some of the books.

"Yeah," Stephen replies, "I was on Team 20 with you and Ashton Cantaloupe." He picks up the rest of the books off the snowy ground.

"How's Zyuquesne?"

"I think it's nice. I live at St. Pam's."

"Nice residence hall. I lived there in my freshman year." Unknown to Toni, the shuttle is about to depart from the campus.

"Thanks for helping me with these books," Stephen says. "Wish I had a new bag…"

"Look," Toni starts, "I'll give you an old bag of mine. That way, you won't trip and fall along with those books!"

"W-wow, thanks!" Stephen and Toni get up off the ground, and the books are recovered.

"You're welcome. 'Bout to study?"

"Yeah, the finals start on Monday. Well, thanks for your help, Toni." Stephen heads back to St. Pam's.

"See ya later." Toni turns around and the shuttle is gone! "Oh no!" he shouts as he dramatically drops his coffee.

CHAPTER FIFTEEN

Toni, after realizing the shuttle left him behind on the way to the Christmas Ball, immediately springs into action, attempting to find another way to Stallion Square.

"Pardon me," Toni says to a woman walking back to Consumption Hall, "do you have a car?"

"Yeah," the woman replies. "Why do you ask?"

"I'm trying to get to the Christmas Ball. Shuttle left me behind…"

"Too bad." The woman walks away from Toni, her footsteps become imprinted onto the snow that sends the blue bricks of B-Walk shivering.

"That was unsurprising," Toni says to himself. "I gotta think of a way to get there!" A-ha! I know who to call!" Toni sends a text to (087)-893-3214 saying, "Hi, can you pick me up at Orbs and McPherson? Gotta go to the Xmas Ball."

"On my way. See you soon," the recipient replied.

"I hope she can get here ASAP!" Toni says. "I can't miss the Ball! Michelle'll be pissed!" Toni starts to shuffle through the snow of B-Walk, heading for Orbs and McPherson, which, by pure convenience, isn't too far of a walk.

Toni puts his crosses his arms together, trying to combat the cold weather sending shivers down his spine.

"I'm almost there," Toni quivers as he sees a street sign saying "Orbs Avenue." He trips and falls into the snow, causing the knee of his pants earning a wet spot for a job well done. A purple minivan pulls up in front of Toni, and the window comes down like a curtain at a play.

"Yo, Toni!" the voice touts from inside the minivan.

"It's about time you got here!" Toni replies. "I didn't know you got a new car, Debbie."

"Not mine," Deborah says, "it's Mom's. Come on, get in! Freezin' out here!"

"Thanks for the lift." Toni gets in the car and puts on his seatbelt. Remember, folks, safety first!

"Okay, how did you miss the shuttle? You were right there!"

"This freshman's books fell on the ground. As I helped him, the shuttle snuck away."

"I guess being a Good Samaritan has its perks, huh?"

"Understatement of the year, sis. We're almost there."

Deborah stops the minivan right in front of the Charity Hotel, where the ushers wait for their next orders to be barked.

"Thanks again," Toni says.

"You're welcome," Deborah replies. "Have fun." Toni gets out of the minivan and Deborah drives off.

Toni sprints inside of the hotel, aiming for the ballroom, where the dance is being held hostage at.

62

"I think that's the room," Toni says, hearing the music blare from across the hallway and lobby. He walks into the ballroom, full of students and staff dancing like maniacs.

"Alright, alright," the DJ says. "Coming up next is gonna be a classic. You know what that means: a slow jam!"

"Toni!" Michelle yells across the ballroom! She and Toni start running towards one another, culminating in a hug. Joey and Reagan also spot Toni as well, walking to him, conserving their energy.

"I couldn't miss out on this," Toni says to Michelle.

"You've got perseverance!" Michelle replies with a smile emerging.

"I'm surprised you got here," Reagan says. "Someone gave you a lift?"

"Yeah, my sister did." Toni answers.

"I knew you'd make it," Joey claims. "After all, he *is* a made man!"

"You were drinking your sorrows out at the thought of Toni not showing up," Reagan replies, elbowing Joey on his arm.

"That's not true," Joey says as he drinks another cup of sparkling cider.

"Well, we're glad you made it," Michelle says to Toni. "Oh, yeah! A slow jam's 'bout to play. Would you like to dance?"

"I'd love to," Toni replies, smiling as he took Michelle's hand.

The two stepped onto the dance floor. Toni places his hands on Michelle's hips, caressing them like a mother and her newborn child; and Michelle wraps her arms around Toni like a present on Christmas.

"This my first time," Toni whispers to Michelle as they dance."

"Really," Michelle asks. "I'm surprised."

"Yeah. But, I couldn't have found a better person to dance with than you for my first time."

"Aww…" Michelle's arms get tighter around Toni. The sensation feels eternal as Michelle and Toni dance together, with the pale moonlight shining onto them for this special evening. After all, it takes two to tango for such an occasion.

CHAPTER SIXTEEN

One week has passed since the Christmas Ball, with the Finals Week shifting into turbo at Zyuquesne University. As the students finished up their tests, the campus starts to become emptier than a cash-grab sequel to a well-beloved movie that was fine standalone. Toni sits inside the lobby of Gowers, playing a game on his phone. Michelle arrives inside the lobby, wearing a pea coat, turtleneck, skirt and boots, carrying two bags.

"You're leaving," Toni asks Michelle as he stands up, putting away the phone.

"Yeah, I finished my finals," Michelle answers. "You're not done with yours?"

"Got one more to go, and then it's over."

"Then what're you doing here?"

"Killing some time. I have twenty minutes before I take it. If you have any time, can we talk?"

Michelle checks her phone, and the time says "2:40." "Yeah, I have a few minutes before Mom arrives."

"Going on vacation?"

"Mm-hmm! My family and I are going to Satchel Ridge, best ski resort in the state!"

"Sounds like fun!"

"You betcha!"

"There's something else on my mind…"

65

"What is it, Toni?"

"I, um, just want to say that, um, you mean the world to me. And… I want to take things to the next level." Toni starts to blush, wary of his stammering.

"Me, too." Michelle's cheeks redden like blood on the dance floor. "Toni… I love you!" She walks closer to Toni, and Toni walks closer to her.

The two gaze into each other's eyes, beaming at each other like sunlight reflecting off the glass of a skyscraper. They close their eyes and their lips embrace for the first time. Michelle and Toni's hug grows tighter and tighter, unwilling to let go, feeling everlasting.

A car beeps outside, interrupting their moment.

"Looks like my Mom's here," Michelle says to Toni as she takes her bags.

"Bye, Michelle," Toni says. "I love you."

"Love you, too. See ya next semester." Michelle walks out of Gowers with her bags, strutting to her mother's car with a grin on her face. Toni starts walking to Prayer Hall, where his last final is at. A bright smile appears on his face, knowing that there is somebody by his side, no matter what or where.

Acknowledgements

"First and foremost, I would like to thank Sarah Gethers, Jeff Nix, Mikayla Hazy and Leah McKown for helping me make my vision come to life. Your input for the play we did was excellent, and I managed to incorporate that into the story. Without you, I don't know where the story could have gone.

Thanks, Mom! Your ideas for what could happen in the story really gave a ton of thought on where I should go. When we talked about Chapter Twelve, you brought out a lot of amazing concepts, and that level of passion is amazing. Thanks again for giving me those tips for the book. I would also like to thank my brothers and my dad for having my support as I continue to write.

In addition, I would also like to thank the following: Dr. Tyra Good, Dr. Selena Marshall, Dr. Boodoo, Marc Grandillo, the Duquesne Program Council, Joseph Patrick, Essence Criswell, Delta Sigma Theta, Steven and James Carter, Andrew Lowery, Mrs. Creighton, Ms. Lindsey, Dr. Holley, Mr. Patterson, Mr. Stys, Megan Toomer, Kameron Simmons, Meghan Hanlon, Killian Bozo, Alexa Brightman, Kristina Celeste, Eleanor Duong, Mimi and Loretta Dougherty, Lauryn Taylor, Megan McGann, Imani Chisom, Alex, Tanner, Kanyon, Armand, Sarah Ssemakula, UAS, Katie Gordon, Gianna, Alia, Horace, Marco Acvedo, Jill Jeffrey, Father Bill, Annarita, Ebony Women, the International Students Organization, Megan Garret, Sean Frankenfield, Mr. Kane, Ms. Geese, Jamar, Stanley, Patrick, Tim, and that's it! Thanks again!

About the Author

Makeem White is a sophomore at Duquesne University, majoring in Digital Media Arts. He is a writer and artist, penning and illustrating *Let Your Emotions Explode* and *The Semester Strikes Back*. He grew up in the Larimer neighborhood of Pittsburgh with his mother, father, and his two brothers. Makeem has been through a lot of hardships over the years, but he never gives up when the going gets tough. He likes to write, draw, and play video games. Makeem also has autism, however, he has never made that an excuse for any of his shortcomings. He still writes to this day.

Art

Gallery

THE ADVENT OF ROMANCE

"The art that you're about to see are drawings that I made during the process of writing *The Advent of Romance*. Keep in mind that not all sketches are created equal. I hope you enjoy seeing the art I've made over the past few months. Cheers!"

-Makeem

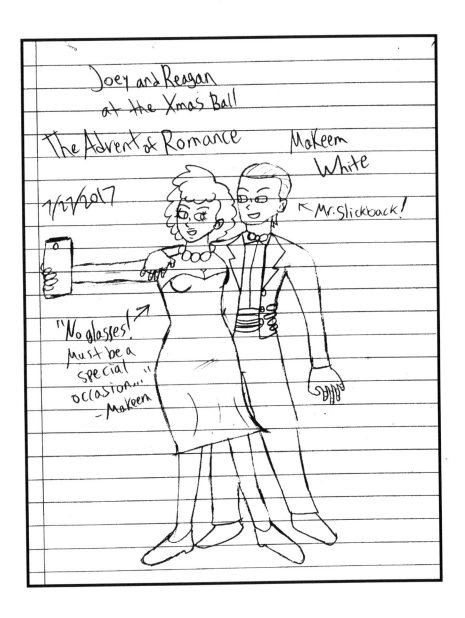

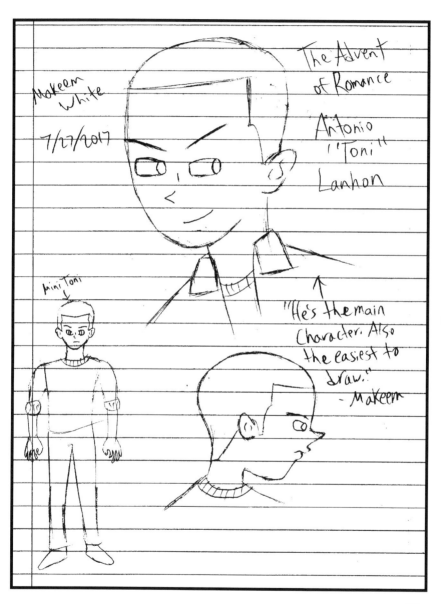

Makeem
White

7/27/2017

The Advent
of Romance

Antonio
"Toni"
Lanhon

Mini Toni

"He's the main
Character. Also
the easiest to
draw."
- Makeem

71

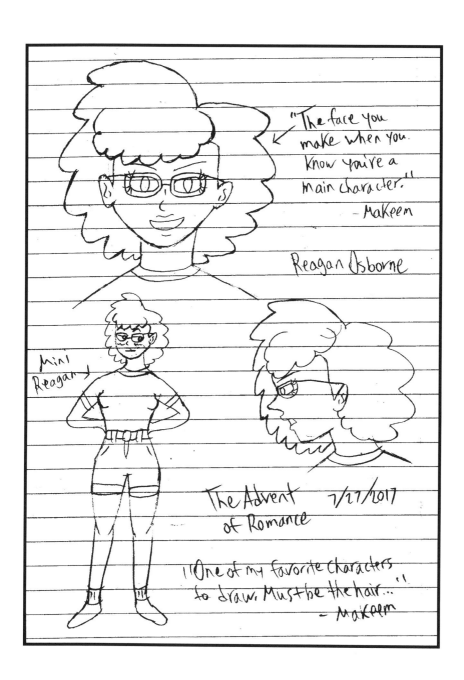

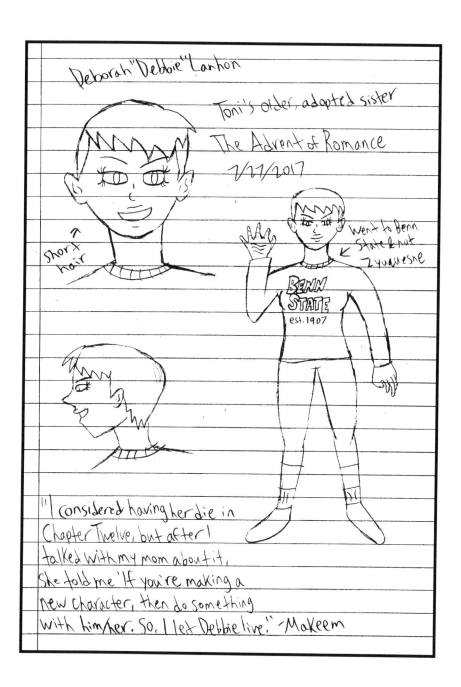

Deborah "Debbie" Lanhon

Toni's older, adopted sister

The Advent of Romance
7/27/2017

Short
hair

Went to Benn
State & not
Duquesne

BENN
STATE
est. 1907

"I considered having her die in
Chapter Twelve, but after I
talked with my mom about it,
she told me 'If you're making a
new character, then do something
with him/her. So, I let Debbie live." -Makeem

THE ADVENT OF ROMANCE

(MANUSCRIPT IN PROGRESS!)

DO YOU UNDERSTAND WHAT HEARTBREAK FEELS LIKE?

78

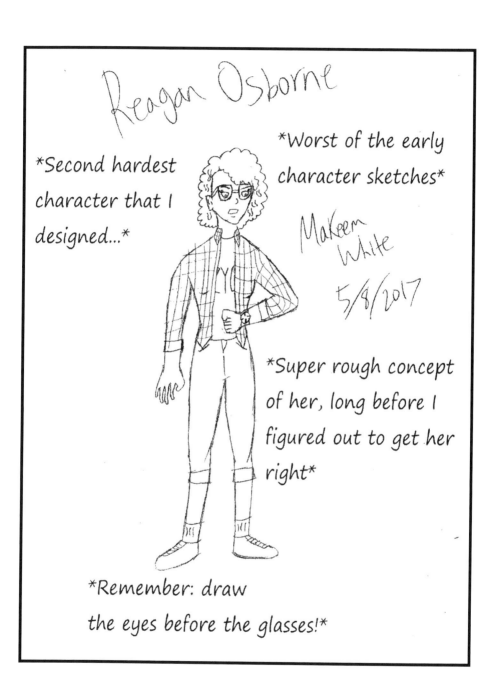

Reagan Osborne

Worst of the early character sketches

Second hardest character that I designed...

Makeem White
5/8/2017

Super rough concept of her, long before I figured out to get her right

Remember: draw the eyes before the glasses!

Originally a part of Alpha Beta Cruton, but idea was scrapped. The cardigan she wears is Reagan's.

Antonio "Toni" Lanhon

Looks more "boyish

Makeem White
5/8/2017

Zyuquesne
Program
Council!

*The ZPC was going
to be a plot point for
Toni, but was scrapped*

The Advent of Romance   Reagan Osborne sans Glasses!!   Makeem White 2/16/2017

YUQUESNE

85

Very early drawing of Toni

Initially had wavy hair, realized he looked too similar to me, so I changed it.

Also, he wore stripes like me.

89

Joey Fibonacci

*Long before I got a
handle on how he should
look...*

Makeem
White
5/9/2017

*Early version of Joey
was a more jock-ish
appearance*

He skipped leg day...

Stephen Gorter

The Advent of Romance

Makeem White 7/28/2017

"Based off a great
Childhood friend of
mine. He's also quite
the artist himself!"
        - Makeem

"I don't draw braided
hair often, but when
I do, I give it all I
got!" - Makeem

The Advent of Romance

Makeem White 7/28/2017

Paul Edward Summers, Jr. AKA "PJ"

DUDE! RANGER

"He's based on one of the kindest people I know. By coincidence, his name is also 'PJ'!" - Makeem

94

Prototype of cover art

*Rough takes
on the cast
of characters*

*Some elements
carried over to final:
Michelle's dress &
Joey's jersey*

95

96

Makeem White   August 16, 2017

Check Out These Titles From Yours Truly:

Made in the USA
Columbia, SC
16 September 2017